945

12 20
7/87

Date Due			
JUN 2 '87	MAY 27 90		
JL 13 '87	EP 11 '		
FEB 23 '88	MAY 07 '		
JUN 2 '88			
APR 19 '89			
JL 10 '89			
AUG 17 '89			
APR 25 '90			
NOV 17 '90			
MAY 24 '94			
JUN 21 '94			
APR 24 '9			

How To Draw The
CIRCUS

Written & Illustrated by **Pamela Johnson**

Watermill Press

Introduction

Ladies and gentlemen and children of all ages—step right up and draw your own circus! It's easy! And it's fun!

Each of the drawings in this book is shown in several simple steps. Just follow each step, adding to your drawing as you go along. Soon you'll have your own circus city beneath the big top.

Are you ready to begin?
Let's go to the circus!

Materials

ERASER

MARKER
MARKER
MARKER

CRAYONS

ou'll need paper, pencils,
nd an eraser to start.
Vhen your drawing looks
he way you want it to,
olor it with crayons,
olored markers, or
ater-color paints.

Drawing
Paper

Remember, the best part
of your drawing is what
you add to it with a little
imagination—so make
your circus friends any
color you want.

Have fun at the circus!

The Parade

Hooray! The circus is in town! It begins with the razzle-dazzle of a great big parade.

Erase line

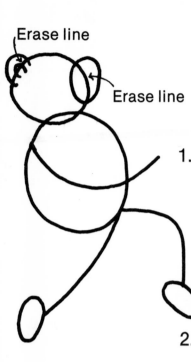

Erase line

1. The drummer is easy to draw. Start with ovals for his head, his body, and his feet. Draw lines as shown for arms and legs.

2. Fill in the arms, legs, and jacket. Then add a mouth, nose, and eyes. Draw an oval for the hand.

3. Draw a circle for the drum and a rectangle for the hat. Now add buttons to the jacket, a stripe to the pants, and a brim and decorations to the hat. Add two little lines to complete each foot.

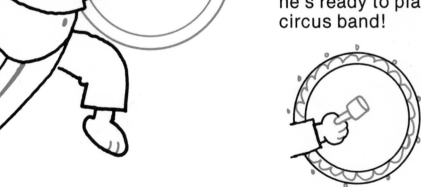

4. Put a drumstick in the drummer's hand. Now he's ready to play in the circus band!

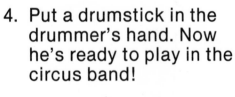

The Circus Train

The circus train is filled with exciting animal acts.

1. Draw a rectangle for each cage. Then add circles for the wheels.

2. Draw the top, bottom, and sides of the cage.

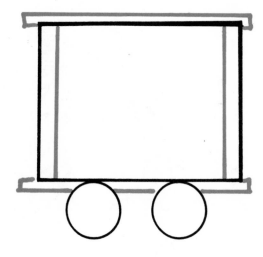

3. Add the bars—we don't want any animals to escape! Draw decorations, too.

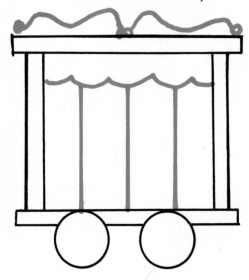

4. Now draw the inside circle for the tire and spokes for the wheels.

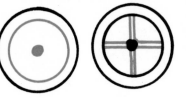

5. When you've finished, add your own circus animal to each cage. Put several cages together to form a circus train, and away we go!

The Big Top

The circus takes place under a tent called the "big top." Everyone helps to put up the tent—even Elmo the Elephant!

Here are two different tents you can draw:

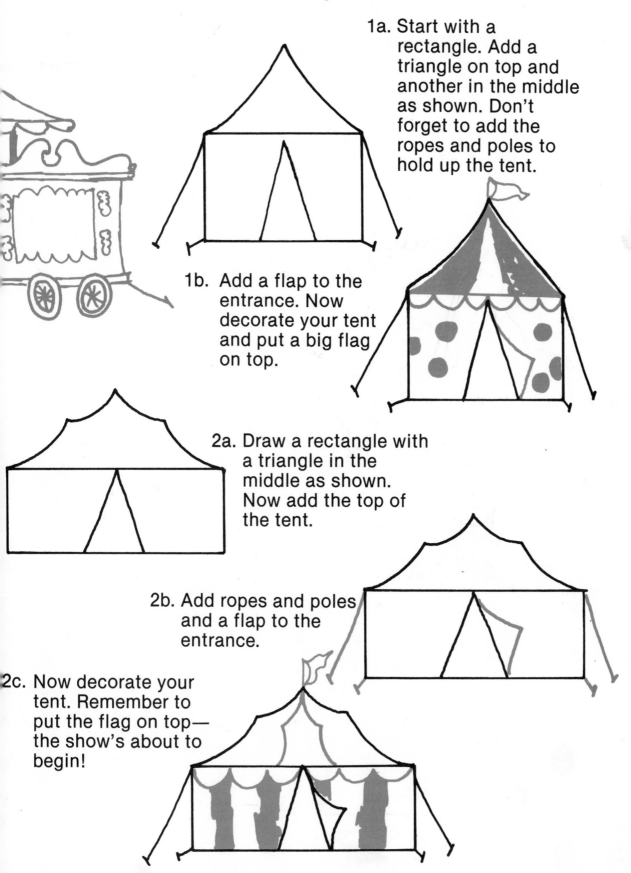

1a. Start with a rectangle. Add a triangle on top and another in the middle as shown. Don't forget to add the ropes and poles to hold up the tent.

1b. Add a flap to the entrance. Now decorate your tent and put a big flag on top.

2a. Draw a rectangle with a triangle in the middle as shown. Now add the top of the tent.

2b. Add ropes and poles and a flap to the entrance.

2c. Now decorate your tent. Remember to put the flag on top— the show's about to begin!

9

Leroy the Lion

Grrowl! Leroy the Lion sounds scary! His trainer must be kind and gentle to make Leroy do his tricks.

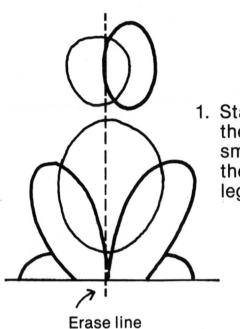

1. Start with an oval for the body and two smaller-sized ovals for the head. Add the hind legs as shown.

Erase line

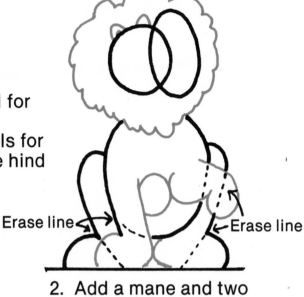

Erase line

Erase line

2. Add a mane and two ears. Then draw the front paws. Add a small circle where the chest should be.

3. Draw the lion's face. Don't be afraid to make him fierce—he won't bite you!

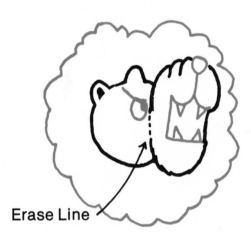

Erase Line

4. Add the tail. Then complete the lion with tiny lines at the tips of his paws.

When you've finished, draw a platform for the lion to stand on.

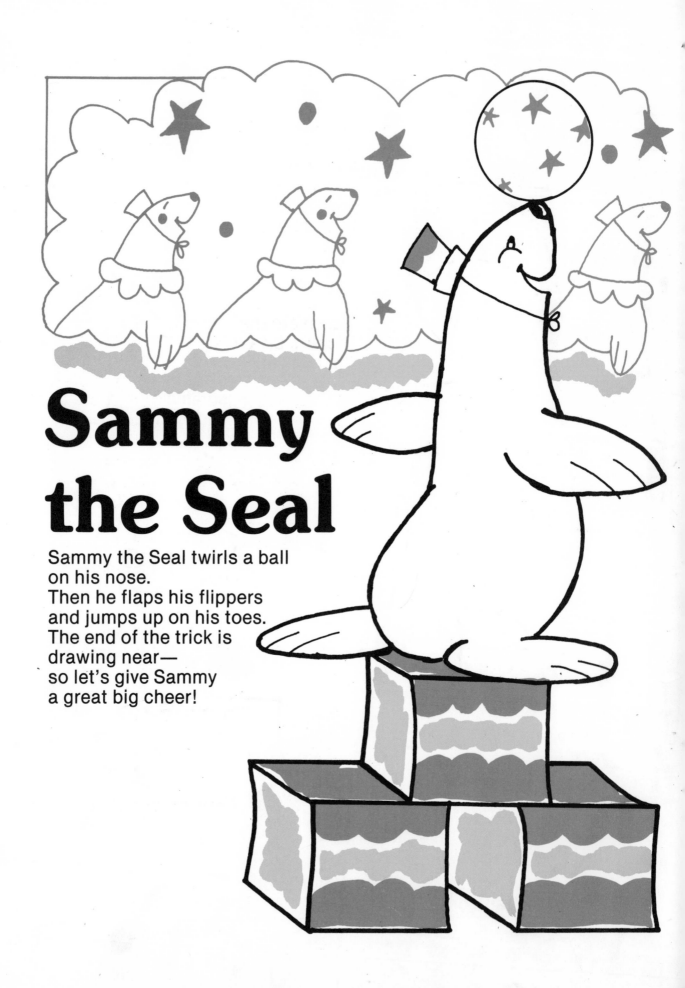

Sammy the Seal

Sammy the Seal twirls a ball
on his nose.
Then he flaps his flippers
and jumps up on his toes.
The end of the trick is
drawing near—
so let's give Sammy
a great big cheer!

1. Start with an oval and add the long, pointed shape as shown for the body. Then add lines for the flippers.

2. Complete the flippers by adding "hands" and "feet."

Erase line

Erase line

3. Draw the seal's face. Then add his costume, a ball for him to balance on his nose, and a box for him to stand on.

Elmo the Elephant

Everyone loves Elmo the Elephant! This great big fellow can do lots of tricks. Elmo loves to balance himself on his hind legs. He likes to march in the circus parade, too.

Elmo eats peanuts, popcorn, and other goodies. But guess what? Like all elephants, Elmo *really* loves fruit. So toss him an apple, sometime!

1. Start with a circle for the body and an oval for the head. Add a line for the trunk and a line for the ear. Then add all four legs.

2. Add toenails on all four feet. Then complete the trunk. Add the blanket and feather hat.

line

Erase line

3. Draw the elephant's face. Be sure to make his ear wavy!

Erase line

4. Now decorate your elephant any way you like. Draw a big platform for him to stand on.

Up we go, Elmo!

Taffy the Tiger

Taffy the Tiger is a circus "big cat."
She is dangerous to train, but lots of
fun to watch.

1. Start with an oval for
the body and a
smaller-sized oval for
the head. Add lines for
the front and hind
legs. Then draw two
small ovals for the
front paws.

2. Draw the ears.
Then finish the
paws and add
a tail.

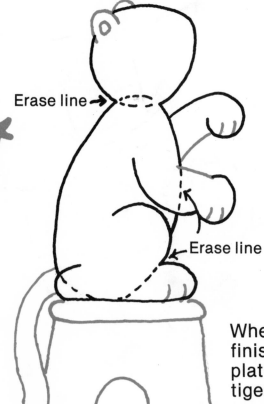

Erase line →

← Erase line

3. Draw the
tiger's face
and fill in the
striped
markings.

When you've
finished, draw a
platform for the
tiger to stand on.

Clowns! Clowns! Clowns!

Here come the clowns! With their painted faces and colorful costumes, they're sure to make you laugh.

Here are a few funny faces you can draw:

1. Start with a circle, an oval, and a few curved lines for the nose, mouth, and ears.

2. Add the eyes. Then fill out the mouth and decorate the cheeks.

3. Complete your clown's face with a wacky hairdo, a silly hat, and whatever else you like. Be creative and make 'em laugh!

Jolly the Juggler

Jolly is a juggling clown. He can juggle lots of things in the air—without dropping a single one!

1. Start with these basic shapes for the head, the body, and the feet.

2. Add a shirt, a vest, a bowtie, and big baggy trousers. Draw two small ovals for the hands.

Erase line

3. Decorate your costume any way you like. Then draw some balls flying through the air. Add lines around each one to show motion. Add details to the hands and feet.

4. Now draw the face of your juggling clown. Don't be afraid to experiment! Use your imagination and have fun!

21

Waddles the Wonder Do

Dogs can do lots of circus tricks. They can walk on their hind legs. They can ride on the backs of galloping horses. They can even jump through hoops—just like Waddles the Wonder Dog!

22

Here are two different dogs you can draw:

1a. Draw the vest and the hind legs as shown. Add the head, the neck, the feet, and the tail.

1b. Draw two ovals for the paws and make wavy lines around the head, legs, and tail for a "poodle" look. Add a collar, too.

1c. Now draw your poodle's face and the hoop she is holding in her mouth. Add details to her hands.

Head

2a. Draw an oval for the body and two smaller-sized ovals for the head. Add the legs as shown.

2b. The dotted lines show you where to erase. Add ears and tiny curved lines to complete the paws.

2c. Draw your dog's face, tail and markings as shown.

Now jump, Waddles! Jump!

Benny the Trapeze Bear

Who floats through the air
with the greatest of ease?
Why, it's Benny the Bear
on the flying trapeze!

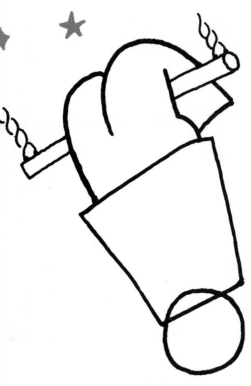

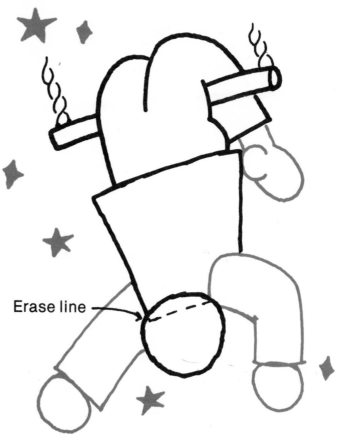

1. Start with the basic shapes for the head and body. Add curved lines for the legs. Then add the trapeze bar.

Erase line

2. Draw the arms, the hands, and one foot as shown.

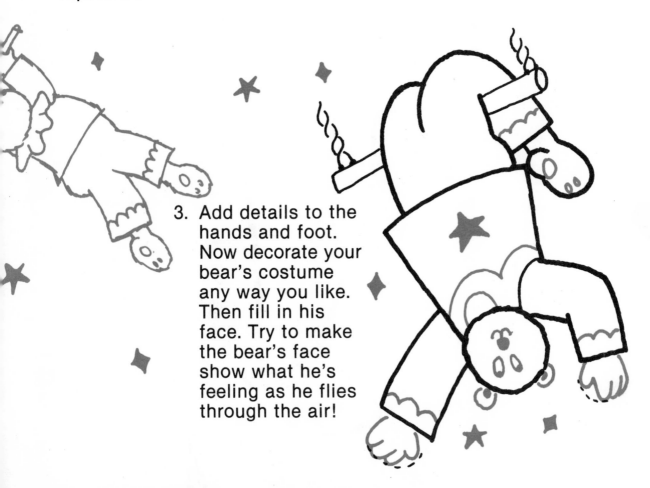

3. Add details to the hands and foot. Now decorate your bear's costume any way you like. Then fill in his face. Try to make the bear's face show what he's feeling as he flies through the air!

The Tightrope Walker

This clown prances gracefully across the thin wire. With parasol in hand, he must balance himself on the tightrope, high in the air!

1. Start with an oval for the body and another oval for the head. Add the arms, legs, hands, and feet as shown.

Erase line

2. Add the shirt and overalls.

3. Add details to his hands and feet. Fill in the details of the clown's costume. Then draw his face. Be creative!

4. When your clown is complete, draw a parasol for him to hold.

Monkey See, Monkey Do!

Monkeys can imitate people. What are these silly monkeys doing?

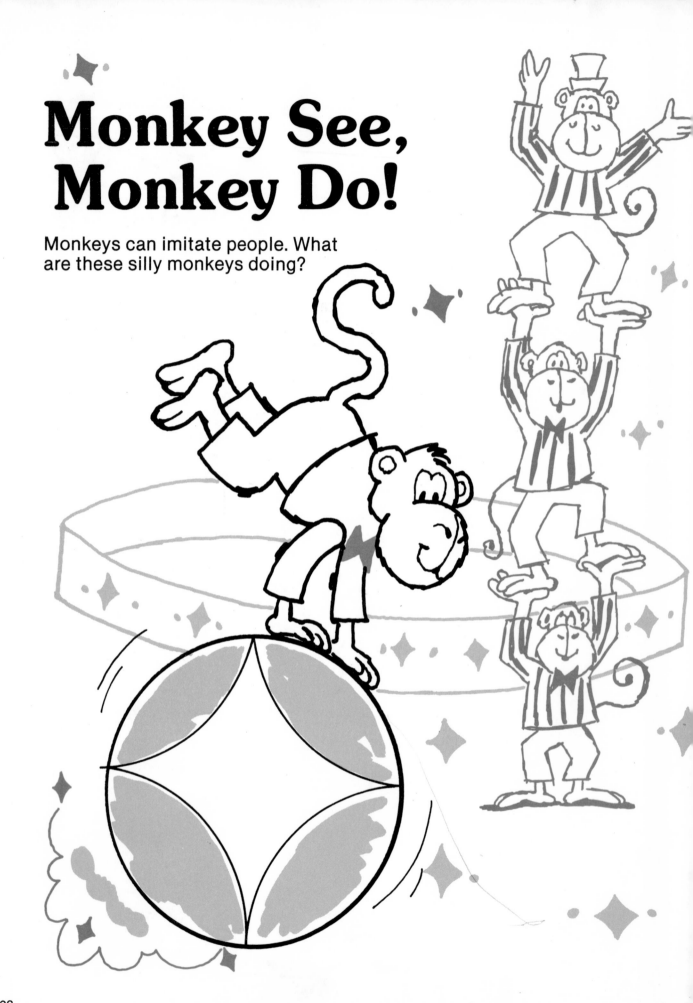

1. Start with an oval for the body and two smaller-sized ovals for the head. Add lines for the arms and legs as shown.

2. Add the ears and a tail. Then fill in the arms, the legs, and your monkey's costume.

Erase line

Erase line

3. Add the hands and the feet.

4. Now give your monkey a funny face!

When you've finished, draw a ball for the monkey to play with!

Circus Snacks

Here are some things you can eat at the circus. Can you name them?

1. _____

2. _____

3. _____

4. _____

5. _____

(Answers: 1. Popcorn; 2. Cotton Candy; 3. Ice Cream; 4. Hot Dog; 5. Soda.)

The Circus Ring

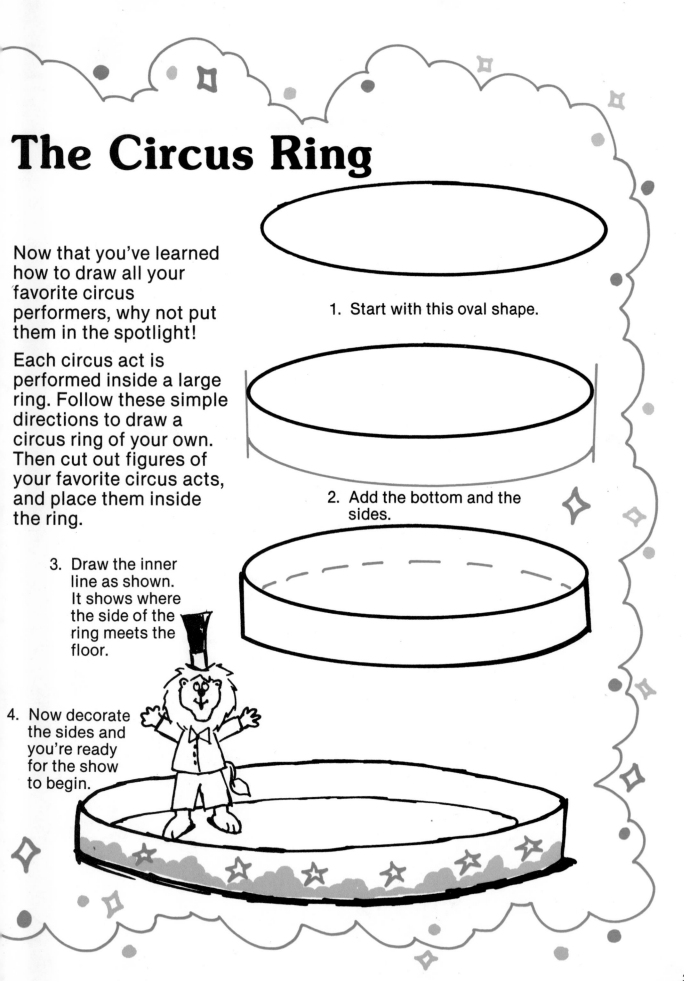

Now that you've learned how to draw all your favorite circus performers, why not put them in the spotlight!

Each circus act is performed inside a large ring. Follow these simple directions to draw a circus ring of your own. Then cut out figures of your favorite circus acts, and place them inside the ring.

1. Start with this oval shape.

2. Add the bottom and the sides.

3. Draw the inner line as shown. It shows where the side of the ring meets the floor.

4. Now decorate the sides and you're ready for the show to begin.